A ROOKIE BIOGRAPHY

DANIEL BOONE

Man of the Forests

By Carol Greene

CHILDRENS PRESS ®

CHICAGO

This book is for Jane Caudill.

Daniel Boone (1734-1820)

LIBRARY OF CONGRESS
Library of Congress Cataloging-in-Publication Data

Greene, Carol.
    Daniel Boone : man of the forests / by Carol Greene
        p.   cm. — (A Rookie biography)
    Summary: A biography of explorer and pioneer Daniel Boone.
    ISBN 0-516-04210-6
    1. Boone, Daniel, 1734-1820—Juvenile literature. 2. Pioneers—
Kentucky—Biography—Juvenile literature. 3. Frontier and pioneer life—
Kentucky—Juvenile literature. 4. Kentucky—Biography—Juvenile
literature. [1. Boone, Daniel, 1734-1820. 2. Pioneers.] I. Title. II. Series:
Greene, Carol. Rookie biography.
F454.B66G74   1990
976.9'02'092—dc20
[B]
[92]   89-25346
                                                                CIP
                                                                 AC

Daniel Boone
was a real person.
He was born in 1734.
He died in 1820.
He was an explorer.
He helped people settle
the new lands in America.
This is his story.

TABLE OF CONTENTS

Chapter 1

Forest Home

The Pennsylvania forests
stood thick and wild.
Deer, rabbits, and foxes
roamed there.
So did bears—and
so did young Daniel.

Daniel was never afraid
in the forest.
His Indian friends
had taught him how
to take care of himself.

Daniel had many
skills to help him
live in the woods.

He could track and hunt.
He could skin and fix meat.
He could build a fire
and wrap himself
in tree bark to keep warm.

Squire Boone (top left) had a blacksmith's shop.

Daniel's father, Squire,
had a blacksmith's shop.
There Daniel learned
to work with metal.
He could fix his own
rifle and traps.

In all, Daniel had
ten brothers and sisters.
He had a good friend
called Henry Miller.
But he felt happiest
alone in the forest.

Once his mother said
Daniel must stay home.
Many people were catching
smallpox, a bad disease.
Sarah Boone wanted
her children to be safe.

But Daniel hated
being stuck at home.
He and his sister Elizabeth
sneaked out one night.
They went to visit a
friend who had smallpox.

Daniel and Elizabeth visited a friend who had smallpox.

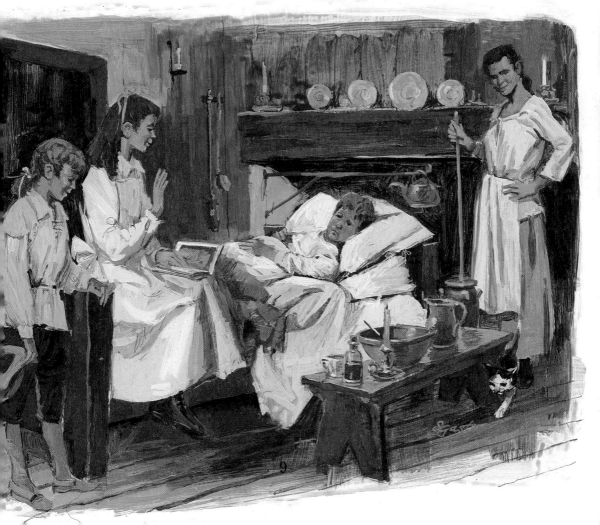

Soon they had smallpox too.
Daniel and Elizabeth were lucky.
They didn't get very sick.
Before long, Daniel was
free to roam again.

Once he stayed out all night.
His mother worried.
Men began to look for him.
They looked for two days.
Then they found Daniel.

He wasn't lost.
Daniel knew
where he was.
He had tracked
and killed a bear.
Now he was eating it.

He told the men
he was sorry
for causing trouble.
Then he gave them
some of his bear meat.

Part of a letter in Daniel Boone's handwriting

Daniel could
read and write.
But his spelling
was poor.
Daniel probably
never went
to school.
That didn't
bother him.

He knew how to make
the forests his home.
That was all
Daniel Boone cared about.

Chapter 2

Yadkin Valley

When Daniel was 15,
his family moved
to Virginia.
Then they moved
to the Yadkin Valley
in North Carolina.

Yadkin Valley,
North Carolina

That was
wild country.
The Boone family
spent their first
winter in a cave
by a river.
When spring came,
they built a cabin.

A log cabin in North Carolina

By then, Daniel earned
money with his hunting.
He was a fine shot.
People said he could shoot
a tiny tick off a bear's nose
from 100 yards away.

When he was 20, he joined
the North Carolina army.
He drove a supply wagon
and worked as a blacksmith.
In 1755, the army fought
French people and Indians.

Young Daniel Boone

CANADA

Wisconsin Territory

Michigan

Illinois

Indiana

Ohio

Lexington •

Kentucky

Tennessee

Alabama

Mississippi

Georgia

New Hampshire

Vermont

Maine

New York

Massachusetts

Rhode Island

Connecticut

New Jersey

Delaware

Maryland

Pennsylvania

Appalachian Mts.

West Virginia

Virginia

Cumberland Mts.

Cumberland Gap

North Carolina

South Carolina

ATLANTIC OCEAN

Kentucky was a faraway and unknown place to the people of colonial North Carolina. The Appalachian Mountains separated Kentucky from the coastal states.

His side lost the fight,
but Daniel wasn't hurt.
He made a new friend, too.
John Finley told Daniel
amazing stories about
a place called Kentucky.

Rebecca Boone

Back home,
Daniel met a
girl named
Rebecca Bryan.
One day, he
pretended to
have an accident.
He cut a big hole
in Rebecca's
beautiful apron.

When she didn't get mad,
Daniel knew that she
was the girl for him.
They got married and
soon had two little boys.
In all, Rebecca and Daniel
had ten children.

Actors play Daniel Boone and Chief Blackfish in an outdoor play called *Legend of Daniel Boone.*

Years went by and
Daniel went on hunting.
When his son James was 7,
Daniel took him hunting.
Soon, he said James was as
good a hunter as he was.

Daniel explored too.
He even went to Florida.
But he kept thinking
about John Finley's stories.
Most of all, he wanted
to explore Kentucky.

At last, in 1769,
he got his chance.

Daniel traveled through the Cumberland Gap (above)
and first saw Kentucky in 1769 (below).

Chapter 3

Kentucky

On May 1, 1769,
Daniel, John Finley,
and some other men
set out for Kentucky.

They rode their horses
over high mountains
and through the
Cumberland Gap.

Buffalo herds grazed on the Kentucky grasslands.

At last they saw the plains.
They saw huge herds of buffalo.

But the Indians in Kentucky
did not want strangers.
It was *their* hunting ground.
They killed one man
in Daniel's group.
They caught Daniel too.
But he escaped.

The other men
went home.
But Daniel stayed.
He hunted and
explored alone.
He went all
the way to the
Ohio River.

**Daniel Boone
hunted alone in the
wilderness of Kentucky**

Daniel
brought
his family
to Kentucky
in 1775.

Daniel was gone for two years.
As soon as he got home,
he was ready to go again.
But he wanted to take
his big family with him
and settle in Kentucky.

That took a while.
In 1773, they started out.
But before they got
to the Cumberland Gap,
Indians killed young James.

So the Boones went to Virginia.
They didn't really settle
in Kentucky until 1775.

By then, Daniel had helped
clear the Wilderness Road
to their new home.
He had helped build
cabins and a fort
at Boonesborough, Kentucky.

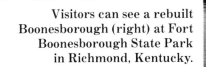

Visitors can see a rebuilt
Boonesborough (right) at Fort
Boonesborough State Park
in Richmond, Kentucky.

The girls were captured by Indians.

But the Indians
were still angry.
In 1776, they
captured Daniel's
daughter, Jemima,
and two other
young girls.

The girls wanted
their families
to find them.
They tried to slow
the Indians down.
They fell off a horse.
They walked slowly.
They tore their
skirts and left the
pieces as markers.

Daniel and others
followed the markers
and rescued the girls.
That was a great day.

Americans cheered when the Declaration of Independence was signed at Philadelphia.

That same year, 1776, the settlers
got news of another great day.
Americans had signed
the Declaration of Independence.
The United States
of America was born.

Daniel was captured
several times
by Indians,
but he always
managed to escape.

Chapter 4

Battles

Battles with
the Indians
went on and on.
They wanted
the settlers
off their
hunting ground.
In 1778,
Shawnee braves
caught Daniel
and other men.

The Indians took the men
all the way to Ohio.
Chief Blackfish liked Daniel.
He decided to adopt him.
He even gave Daniel
a new name—Big Turtle.

But Daniel knew
the Shawnees were going
to attack the fort
at Boonesborough.
He acted happy.
But he was waiting.

At last, he tricked
the Indians and escaped.
He traveled for four days
with almost no food.
But he made it to
Boonesborough.

His family had left the fort.
But others took care of him.
Then they got ready
for another battle.

The settlers fought off the Indians at Boonesborough.

The Indians attacked
the fort for nine days.
They used rifles.
They threw burning torches
and shot burning arrows.
They dug a tunnel.

But rainy weather
helped the settlers.
The fort didn't burn.
The tunnel fell in.

At last, the Shawnees
gave up and left.
In 1779, Daniel
found his family and
brought them home again.
Other settlers came too.

Standing over the body of his son Israel, Daniel keeps fighting.

There would be
many more battles.
People called 1782
the Year of Blood.
Daniel's son Israel
was killed that year.

The Indians did all
they could to keep
their hunting ground.
But they couldn't win.
In 1783, the battles
ended and peace
came to Kentucky.

Portrait of Daniel Boone

Chapter 5

Last Trips

Daniel still hunted.
He owned a lot of land, too.
But he had problems.

Smart lawyers kept
taking him to court.
They tried to prove
he *didn't* own his land.
Most of the time, they won.

The settlers made most of what they used in their daily life. Weaving (top) left), soap making (top right), candle making (bottom left), and basket weaving (bottom right) were important skills.

Years went by.
Daniel had opened
Kentucky for settlers.
He was famous for that.
But now he had
almost no land left.

By 1799, he was
ready to move on.
The Spanish government
owned land in the west.
They asked him
to come to Missouri.

Daniel (inset) built this log cabin in Missouri.

So Daniel made a big canoe
for his family to travel in.
But Daniel himself walked
all the way to Missouri.
He was 64 years old.

In Missouri, he got land
and brought more settlers.
Then he lost that land, too.

At last, he went
back to the forests.
He hunted and sold furs.
When he was 82, he walked
all the way to Yellowstone.
Then he walked back.

Next, he walked to Kentucky.
He owed money to people there.
He wanted to pay them.
Then he came back
to his son Nathan's house
in Missouri.

Nathan Boone's house in Missouri

Statue of Daniel Boone (left).
A stone memorial marks the graves of
Daniel and Rebecca Boone in
Frankfort, Kentucky (below).

And there the old hunter
got sick and quietly died.
He had lived almost 86
hard and wonderful years.

Important Dates

1734   November 2—Born in Exeter, Pennsylvania, to Squire and Sarah Boone

1751   Moved to Yadkin Valley, North Carolina

1756   Married Rebecca Bryan

1769   Set out for Kentucky

1775   Settled in Kentucky

1778   Captured by Shawnee Indians

1799   Moved to Missouri

1820   September 26—Died in St. Charles, Missouri

INDEX

Page numbers in boldface type indicate illustrations.

PHOTO CREDITS

ABOUT THE AUTHOR

Carol Greene has degrees in English literature and musicology. She has worked in international exchange programs, as an editor, and as a teacher. She now lives in St. Louis, Missouri, and writes full-time. She has published more than eighty books. Other books in the Rookie Biographies series include *Benjamin Franklin, Pocahontas, Martin Luther King, Jr., Christopher Columbus, Abraham Lincoln, Robert E. Lee, Ludwig van Beethoven, Laura Ingalls Wilder, Jackie Robinson,* and *Jacques Cousteau.*